Little Tyke

By Mike Wilson

© 2014

Free Spirit Writers

ISBN: 978-1-291-87057-2

Little Tyke © Mike Wilson

First published 2008 by Free Spirit Writers, Bridlington

Published 2014 by

LODGE
BOOKS

25 South Back Lane
Bridlington
www.lodgebooks.co.uk

Thanks

I would like to thank everyone who has inspired even a single word in this collection. These pieces are written in a variety of voices and only a handful should be taken as the voice of the author himself. Similarly, some of the relationships spoken of by those voices are not those of the author. These poems hopefully express how any boy could respond to a certain set of circumstances. The reaction of the characters to situations revealed in the poems is theirs alone.

Support is acknowledged from members of Bridlington Writers' Group, the National Association of Writers' Groups, other writers and friends, and especially my wife Diane. Particular thanks go to Brian Lister, Sue Lozynskyj, Steve Bowkett and Alison Chisholm, who offered creative observations.

In 2006, *Grandad*, *Our Lass*, *My Dad* and *My Mam* (along with *Playing with Daddy*, which is not included in this collection) were entered in the National Association of Writers' Groups' competition for the best collection of five poems. Judge Alison Chisholm chose them as one of three runners-up out of an entry of 83. She commented: "The juxtaposition of cosy and disturbing makes this set particularly memorable. The poet has captured the voices with intensity and accuracy."

Mike Wilson

Dedication

This book is dedicated to Diane, who lifted the lid of the jack-in-the-box and released me to enjoy a full and rewarding life. We're strong, because we're three: me, you and us.

"Your book captivated me and carried me into a parallel universe – different but so very familiar. That's the magic of poetry!"
Alison Chisholm

"A really clever weave of nostalgia and powerful commentary on some of the problems that kids did and still do face. I like the varied verse forms, which keeps the collection fresh and a pleasure to read from cover to cover."
Steve Bowkett

Little Tyke

Mi Mam's been baking.
She's done jam tarts, lemon curds and 'chissocks.'
They're really cheesecakes
but Mam calls them 'chissocks'
just like Granny does.
Our Lass likes her lemon curds
but me,
I'm a jam tart lad.
Mam's pastry is light and crumbly
and the jam is made from mi Dad's own strawberries
grown down the allotment.
She's put tarts on the windowsill to cool,
and I'm off to nick one,
or two.

Reach in, steady . . .
that's one,
that's two.
Arm out and . . .

Mi Mam's there and she clips my ear'ole.
"I'll knock your block off,
you little tyke."

When I run away she's shouting,
as though she's the Queen of Hearts.

But she's got a big grin on her face.

My Dad

Everyone liked my Dad.
He was a nice bloke,
kind, quiet; he'd give you his last shilling.
He'd burn two slices of toast for breakfast
and spread dollops of mi Mam's raspberry jam on them.
His bike was no racer; he got to work on time
just
but he was first to start.

It was hard work at the printers.
His muscles bulged when he lifted formes
to put on the press.
I've read bits of posters printed on his bare arms.

He always gave my Mam a kiss when he went to work,
and another when he came home.

Aye, he were a nice bloke, were my Dad.
He'd ruffle my hair when he passed me on his way out.
"All right, son?" he always asked.
And I always was.

Pity God took him before
I'd finished with him.

My Mam

My Mam knows everything.
She knows it's time to get up when it *is* time to get up.
She knows when I've bunked off school.
Somehow, she knows.

She throws my jumper into the washer and shouts:
"I don't know why you have to lark in that park!
It's not safe!"
How does she know?

My Mam knows more than David Cameron.
He should listen to her if he wants to run the country better.
My Mam'd tell him.

And heaven help the butcher telling her which meat to buy.
My Mam knows more about meat than anybody.
Which is funny, because she won't eat it.
Nothing with a face, she says.
I suppose she knows something we don't.

I asked my Dad where I came from,
to see if he knew,
and he says "Ask your Mam!"

And she says: "Bridlington,"
which wasn't what I expected.
So maybe she doesn't know everything.

They probably didn't have sex lessons in her day.

Grandad

My Grandad's face has a big red nose stuck on the front
and his ears remind me of shed doors.
When I ask him where his hair went
he chuckles and rubs his fingers on the top of his head.
"I needed more space for brain," he says,
and crosses his fingers to show it's true.

And he says the Queen wanted his teeth for a pearl
    necklace,
but even if he does cross his fingers,
I know he's fibbing.

Without his teeth, his face collapses.
He says he borrowed it from a gargoyle.

Grandad doesn't run any more;
he reckons he's saving himself, but won't tell me what for.

My Grandad can sing The Beatles and The Rolling Stones,
and he's taught me how to spit in the harbour.

When we play dominoes I beat him sometimes
even though he's the best player in the pub.

Grandad smiles when he watches Our Lass and other pretty
    girls.
His eyes light up.

But if he's with Grandma his whole face smiles
and when he kisses her
her eyes shine too.

Our Lass

I'll give 'er 'er due,
she does practise.
I've come home for my football
and the 'ouse is shakin',
an' the ornaments rattlin',
an' the dog 'owlin' in the corner at the music.
You wouldn't believe it to look at 'er,
but she wants to be a ballerina.
I mean, she's too fat now.
What's she goin' to be like when she's ten?
She watches videos of Swan Lake
an' pretends to be Darcey Bussell
kiddin' 'ersen: "I can do that!"
Ma says "She has to have her dreams."
Well, she can 'ave 'em, but it ain't goin' to 'appen.
No way.
Never.
She's more a barrelina,
so, no, I can't see Our Lass being a dying swan.

I'm off to play footie now,
I'm practising for Man U.

School photo

Good job the sun's shining.
It's school photo day.
Mi Mam's washed mi hair –
to get the rats' tails out, she says –
and put a dollop of mi Dad's Brylcreem on
before she combed it.

She says I've to smile.
I don't know why.
No-one's going to see the photo.
We can't afford one
and none of my pals can either.
But because I'm at Grammar School now
Mam thinks it's important.
I've to be on mi best behaviour
and do exactly what I'm told.
"And don't screw your eyes up!"

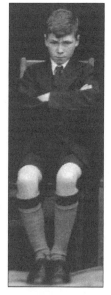

I bet I'm on the front row
showing mi knees.
I'm still wearing short trousers
but some lads will have dropped.

I wish Mum could afford a photo
so in fifty years' time,
I can try to remember who all the lads are,
and maybe see in the boy
the man I have become.

Milly

We're visiting Milly today.
Auntie Gladys says Milly won't have a proper life,
always in a wheelchair.
And nappies.

Mum says she's bearing up.
I know she smiles when she says that,
but you can tell her eyes hurt.

Dad says Milly's a fighter,
even though she can't see us or hear us.

I'm watching her in that tent.
She isn't very big,
and her skin's a funny blue.
Those pipes and tubes
make her look like a monster.

"We're doing everything we can," the doctor says.
Mum reckons they are saving her life.

But I wonder:
What for?

Blood

I don't like blood.
Mi Mam's washing me after football.
"Black as Ace of Spades," she says.
I stand in a bowl of warm water,
and the flannel is melting the mud off mi legs.
But I'd come a cropper in the goalmouth
and teacher's stuck a plaster on mi knee.
Mi Mam gets hold of one end
and yanks it off.
When I see the torn skin
and the leaking blood
I keel over.
Water everywhere.

I hit the kerb round the fire,
so I get another cut — on mi head.

Mam dabs it with the flannel,
shows me the blood,
and mi lights go out again.

Father O'Halley

Father O'Halley's hands were soft and gentle
like those of Our Lord
and I was humbled
to serve on the altar as he said Mass.
At the *Lavabo*
I poured water over his fingers
so they were pure
when he handled the host.
He held the Body of Christ high
for the congregation's awe,
then broke it and ate,
following Jesus's commands.

In his absence
I served another priest,
who told me Father O'Halley
was home in Ireland.

The paper said he'd been blown up
in a house where men
were making bombs for the IRA.

Midnight Mass

Still dreamy,
we pull on our clothes,
then our coats and scarves,
and go out into the dark.
That's the strangest thing:
going out in the night.
We walk down the road to the short cut over the playing
    fields,
and onto the grass.
You can't tell it's green; that is weird.

People puff their breath in front of them,
all snuggled into their coat collars.

We go to our usual pew,
not down the centre aisle
where all the posh people are,
but at the side where we can't be seen.
The service is same as Sunday's
but we sing carols, which I like.

When we are outside again, it is still night.
Wishing everyone "A Merry Christmas"
we wander close together across the park.

I have to go to church
but I'm not sure about this faith stuff.

On the way home
I keep a lookout in the sky
for Father Christmas.

White balloons

It's near Christmas
and I'm at Charlie's house
helping with the decorations.
Charlie's pa and ma have bought the tree
and we're hanging tinsel and baubles on the branches.
They have a string of little electric lights,
with real small bulbs,
which light up.

Charlie's pa throws a packet of balloons
for us to blow up.
There are all colours.
We puff and blow,
blow and puff,
but can't get them going.
Charlie's pa starts a few off for us
and soon there are balloons everywhere.

I have two long white ones,
and Charlie's pa shouts:
"Look, Sally, white balloons!"

There's a crash in the kitchen.
I think she's dropped some plates.

I've no idea why.

Am I bovvered?

I lark abou' a' school,
and always play the fool.
        Am I bovvered?
Yeah, I know I'll never pass
'cos I mess abou' in class.
        Bu' am I bovvered?
So I fail your bloody tests
and I'm rude to all your guests.
        Am I bovvered?
Do you fink I really care
that you don't like my hair?
        Am I bovvered?
So I called that teach a slag
'cos she grabbed me only fag.
        Why you bovvered?
Am I the only one around
chucking rubbish on the ground?
        Why you bovvered?
So you fink my mates are mugs
bein' hooked on stupid drugs.
        Should I be bovvered?
You say I'll soon regre' i'?
Well, all my life is shi'.
        Do you fink I'm bovvered!

Brambling

We're brambling in Boynton Woods today.
Mi Mam's bramble pies are fantastic
but mi Dad whispers that her custard's so thick
the English trampoline team could practise on it.
Me, I like it like that.
Anyway, brambling's good fun,
even though it's not so warm out now.
Mi Mam has a basket
and we all grab as many berries as we can.
The best ones are always just out of reach,
and mi Dad's shoes are blathered in mud
after slipping into a ditch.
But these biggest, fattest, oozy-juicingest berries
are too nice to be in a pie,
so I pinch them
and squash them between mi tongue
and the roof of mi mouth,
the juice bursting down mi throat.
Smashing!

Fire

My Dad hates fire.
He still makes one
so my Mam doesn't have to do it.
He puts an old *Daily Mirror* on the mat
when he kneels down.
He clears the ashes and chucks them in the dustbin.
Old newspapers rolled into sticks go in t' fireplace first,
then chopped wood,
then coal.
He flicks his lighter
and the paper burns.
To help the flames
he stretches one sheet of newspaper to close the fireplace
    over.
Sometimes that sheet catches fire,
and Dad drops it, sharpish.
When the fire's well alight, Dad adds more coal.

Dad hates fire,
because in the war he was a fireman.
He tried to drag his best friend out
after a Wimpey crash-landed and burned at
    Lossiemouth.
When he pulled hard to get him free,
the bloke's arm came off.

So he hates fire.
I hate it too.

Watch the birdie!

Through squinting eyes
I "watch the birdie!"
A scowl questions
its existence,
that I'm posed -
willing or not -
on the Town Hall lawn.

My baby curl droops,
no longer a feature for admiration.
An arm protects my teddy bear
as he too waits to see what happens next.

Was I really that surly sullen child?

Laundry field

Every Friday afternoon
I have to go to Convent
to learn the catechism
off the Sisters of Mercy.

Two lads ask: "Where yer going?"
I say "Convent,"
get punched in the face,
then shoved into the brambles.

After they've run off, I go home, bleeding.

I'm learning to be a Catholic
but I'm not turning the other cheek.

Affection

Not one to give affection is my Dad.
He doesn't understand my need for care
so all he does is shout and scream and swear

that now I'm twelve I know I must be bad.
My life is getting more than I can bear.
Not one to give affection is my Dad

now Mum has gone. But secretly I'm glad
she had her chance to find a new affair.
Despite the fact he's now a millionaire,
not one to give affection is my Dad.

Equality

We did "Equality" yesterday.
Dad says he's all in favour.
He says he's glad women are free and equal
and after Mum's washed up,
made the beds,
brought the washing in
  and ironed it,
  especially his best shirt for church,
fetched the coal in,
built up the fire,
baked the bread,
  and Sunday's scones and jam tarts,
she can meet him in the pub
and go to the match
if she wants.

The postman brings the future

He brings the 'O' Level results. I fail.
He invites me to National Service. I go.
He carries the letter that sends me abroad.
This envelope brings the message that my Dad has died.
This, that Mum is in hospital.
And when I think the postman can do no worse,
he brings me this.

And my future ends with your "Dear John."

The Apprentice's Printer's Pie

The blokes at work made me a pie today.
They wrapped it up with strong and sturdy string.
It seemed too heavy to be a normal pie;
they said the pie would go with anything.

I took it home and gave it to my mum.
She smiled when told who'd given it to me:
"We'll have it for our tea tonight then, son,"
and hid the pie. She wouldn't let me see.

When teatime came I loved that apple pie;
with custard made by Mum, it tasted good.
My portion seemed to have no weight at all
but I was pleased to eat their printer's pud.

They laughed at me next day. I wondered why.
They told me then what's really printer's pie.*

*Printer's pie is a jumble of type, usually after it has been
dropped. Printer's type is composed mainly of lead, that's why
it's so heavy.

Granny Barr's

Granny Barr lived at Cranswick,
a bus ride away.
She and Grandad lived in a cottage
with a huge garden,
with sheds, chickens and rhubarb.
It was fun prowling through the long grass
playing cowboys and Indians
or searching for hidden treasure.
In spring we found fluffy yellow chicks,
in autumn fallen apples
Mum took home to make pies with.
In summer the evenings lasted for ever
but in winter it was draughty
in their smelly outside lavvy.

Believing

I've stopped believing in things,
especially Father Christmas.
I should have worked it out myself really.

As for the Tooth Fairy,
well, that's all right for lasses and little kids.

Believing in Jesus is OK,
but I'm not too sure about God.
The sisters at Convent say he listens.
Maybe he does but he doesn't do owt about it.
I prayed that our lass didn't die with scarlet fever.
But she did.
So I don't want to believe now.

I still don't like the dark
and in bed I keep the light on
in case the bogeyman grabs me.

○

How I admired it
while I was in the bath:
My first pubic hair.

The last Friday

Last Friday of the month
is haircut day – half price for boys.
Mi Mam takes me to Slasher Smith's in town.
He is a big chap,
bulging,
with a pinny round the equator of his waist.
Sailors and nudes dance on his arms
and his moustache twitches
from the effects of the bombing.
There are two styles offered:
Short and shorter.
His scissors slash and cut and flash
round his customers' heads.
Hair of brown and black and grey and white
snowflake to tatty linoleum.
When he calls "Next!"
mi Mam pushes me forward
to be enveloped in a grubby sheet
and I sit swathed in this flowing gown
on a box in his chair.
"Short back and sides?" he shouts at Mam.
"No, just a trim, Mr Smith."
His glower makes me cower deeper into the chair.
I can count the hairs on his belly,
nearly taste the pomade,
and practically choke on his breath.

When he's finished and Mam is paying the shilling
I wonder why he doesn't ask me
if I'd like something for the weekend.

Paper-boy

Got a job as a paper-boy at Smithson's shop.
Six o'clock I've to get up
and be there at half past.
Old Smithson said:
"I'll have no truck with latecomers."
What lorries have to do with it I don't know.

I have a bag stuffed with dailies and magazines.
I'm like a bunch of matchsticks
tied up with a two-ton bag.
But once I'm delivering it gets lighter.

I'm supposed to deliver according to 'the round.'
But at the end of the month
I go to No.103 last
so's I can sneak a look at the pictures
in *Health & Efficiency*.

Hurdy gurdy man

He isn't much to look at,
small, hunched, beaky nosed,
wearing a long black coat that sweeps the road.
Under his wide-brimmed hat,
he's half starved
and can hardly shift his hurdy gurdy.
If I hear him in the street
I leave my plastic Spitfire
and gaze at him through the window.
When he winds that handle
out comes a stirring sound.
It makes my feet curl
and my toes want to dance.
It seems to get right inside me,
fills me up with magic.
I can see leprechauns dancing
in an Irish meadow,
and witches chanting over a smelly brew.
I imagine how it would be to fly
and look down on the town
to see where I live.

After ten minutes he picks up the handles
and trundles off
to give freedom to somebody else's soul.

Sarnies

Mam packs a lunch for me
and at dinnertime
me and the printers
go down to the canteen.
A lass pours tea from a pot
that's exactly the same colour as the tea:
a real dark glossy brown
like well-polished solicitors' boots.
I'm interested in their sandwiches.
One chap has bacon and egg in his,
another has cheese,
and the other apprentice has strawberry jam,
every day.
My Mam does me salmon.
When I tell them that
the men all nod
and wink at each other.
"Aye, we know thi Mam,"
they say
and then laugh.
I don't see what at.
I know it's tuna,
but I'm not off to call
mi Mam a liar,
am I?

One of ours

They come in the night.
No-one will tell us what they are.
We hear their special sound,
an uneven drone
harsher than bumblebees in summer.
Even though the sky is dark
we can see them,
their insides glowing.
Then there's bangs and thumps and crumps
and the sky goes red for a moment.
Mother says: "Someone's copped it."
Then another comes
with a roar and swoosh,
getting closer, then disappearing.
Mother says: "It's OK. It's one of ours."
"Our what?" I ask
as we scramble over the wall
to the safety of Mrs Holmes's cupboard.

A friend lost

I nearly met a friend today.
But harsh words had split us.
The smile on my lips
at seeing him
was dashed
as he remembered,
cast his eyes to the ground,
and drew the anger,
and his resentment,
around him like a cloak.

Another confession

I have another confession to make.
I never really wrote that poem.

At school they thought I had written it.
When teacher said it was good
I was pleased
but in my heart I knew it wasn't mine.
The other boys were chuffed
their names were in the poem
but I couldn't let on.
They stopped braying me because I wrote about them
and I was glad I wouldn't go home bleeding.

Teacher said he'd put my poem in the school book,
the one that came out every year.
He said my poem was a good example
and that he was proud of me.

I felt ashamed I couldn't tell anyone.
My Mum was pleased it had been chosen.
She let me say it was my poem.

Mostly it was hers.
My lie still lingers in that book.

Sorry.

Our shed

My Dad's put a shed in't yard.
He bought it cheap off a bloke at the allotment.
It fell off a lorry, he told me.
It looks good and he's fair trimmed wi' it.
Two days after t'rent man had been
Dad gets a letter from t'council
and Mam read it for him.
Halfway through she starts giggling.
Dad asks her: "What's so funny, lass?"
And she reads out in a pretend posh voice:
"The authority does not permit erections on council
    property."

My Dad hasn't stopped laughing all week.

Woolies

Mi Mam'll be dead chuffed
'cos I've learnt summat today.
She's always on abart learnin'.
Me and Gazza were in Woolies
and he showed me how to nick goodies.
It's easy.
At first I didn't dare
but Gazza says every lad at school
gets free goodies at Woolies.
He kept the lass behind the counter talking
while I snuck past
like a whisper.
I snaffled a packet of chocolate fags first go.
We scarpered.
No-one seemed bothered.
When we were on the harbour,
we ambled past the trawlers with fags in our gobs
pretending to be grown-ups.
It was magic how I felt
'cos now I was a thief like the rest of 'em.
Tomorrow I'm off back to Woolies.
I'll get Mam some sweets
'cos I love her.

Swish

Our John's crying again.
He's been swished at school.
Mam asks him what for.
"Don't know," he mutters.
But he does;
he told me.
At his posh school
they get swished for nowt.
It hurts like mad
when they swish your hand, he says.
Mi Mam tells him he must've done summat.
"No Mam, I didn't," he says.
He doesn't like that school.
He goes by train every day before I have mi breakfast.
Sometimes he gets in when I'm having mi supper.
I feel sorry for him,
but I know I'll have to go next year.
I think it's 'cos Mam wants to boast
"My boys go to a Catholic school,"
and be one up at church.

It's all right for her;
she's not getting swished.

Scrumping

Old Farmer Harvey told us to bugger off today.
Mi Mam would have a fit if she heard him say that.
He's always at communion on a Sunday
and Mam reckons he's a real good Catholic.
He weren't very forgiving when me and Jack
were pinching apples from his orchard.
You should have heard him cuss.
It were worse than I've heard by them soldiers
and my Mam says they should have their tongues cut
    out.
Anyhow we only grabbed a handful.
It weren't as if we had a barrow or owt.
We only just got down that tree in time.
He can't run 'cos of his war wound
so we left him miles behind.

Trouble was
them apples were as bitter and twisted as he was.

Lucozade

After the belly ache and Doctor Brown,
the mad scramble to find pyjamas,
toothbrush and paste, flannel, soap,
and clean pants,
I cling to my Mum's hand
as we wait for the ambulance.
The frantic drive to hospital
rattles my pain
before I suck in that gas
and there's nothing.

I'm glad to see my Dad tonight,
even though I'm groggy.
He's brought me Lucozade.
"Help make you well, son," he says.
"You'll soon be fit as me."
"Thanks, Dad."

Then he gets on his bike
and cycles home.

Eighteen miles.

B-17

My mind soared
at the white plaster moulded B-17.
For a whole hour
my arm flew sorties
over Mannheim and Schweinfurt.
I took off from the dining table
until Mam shoo'd me off
so she could set the table for Christmas dinner.
I landed on the lino runway
under the tree
by the door.
When I'd tired of flying,
I built a castle of all the things in my pillowcase:
new slippers, a pullover for school,
"The Golden Wonder Book for Boys,"
and a paper bag with an orange,
three walnuts and a bar of chocolate.

Carefully, I placed the B-17 on the top
like the star on the Christmas tree.

My sister barged through the door
and my B-17 was destroyed
by enemy action.

My grandmother

Dad's mother is a sombre lady,
black dressed,
squat in her chair in the corner,
next to a bristling fire
guarded by sooted fire irons.
I never see her smile
nor hear a word of praise.
Family visits are a duty,
I can tell;
Dad always sighs
when the door closes behind us.

There's a soldier,
huge framed.
Brightened by fire,
his eyes follow me.
"That's your Grandad," my mother says,
quietly.

But he's not the man who lives with my grandmother,
married her, provided for five small bairns,
as if they were his own.

I think,
it would be nice to see Granny smile,
just once.

Shoes in cupboard

It's a game we play at home.
We clear the table after Sunday tea,
make last week's *Daily Mirror*s into sticks,
tidy up Mam's knitting,
Dad's library books,
our lass's dolls
and my cars,
and then we play.

I can't remember the rules -
if there are any -
but what you have to do is put
the shoes in the cupboard.
It isn't as easy as it sounds
because the rest of the family
try to stop you,
even though they're blindfolded.

My Dad is strong,
my Mam is cuddly,
our lass is all skinny arms and legs,
and then there's me.
I'm littlest.

I have to fight my way past my Dad,
but he picks me up by the braces,
and drops me back on the settee.

If I get past him –
I think he lets me by sometimes on purpose –
mi Mam's in the way.
She just smothers me with her cuddly bosom.
I like that so I don't fight hard to get free.

Our lass plays for real.
She won't let me pass.
But Dad finds a way
and eventually I put the shoes in the cupboard.
It's great fun.

I learn something too:
My Dad's strong, but uses it to help;
my Mam's cuddly, and she lets everyone have their fair
   share;
and our lass is just a daft girl.

But I'm beginning to see
what Johnny Smith has his eye on.

Apprentice

Was *this* what my education had been for:
A broom?

Sines and cosines,
"the square on the hypotenuse of a right-angled triangle
    is equal to the sum of the squares on the two adjacent
    sides,"
quadratic equations, logarithms,
all lost in the battle with the broom.

Amo, amas, amat, amamus, amatis, amant,
or *Ich weiss nicht, was soll es bedeuten, Dass ich so traurig
    bin,*
no help in sweeping floors.

At sixteen,
in the big, wide world they spoke of,
my duty: to clean.

I sweep, remembering how my mother cleans the house.
But this is no spick-and-span council house,
but a dusty floor, a wooden surface
worn away by men's boots.
Clouds of dust bring anguished howls
from Lino ops and compositors.
"Slek the dust, lad, slek the dust."

It's all Greek to me.

Family photo

We all sat in our best:
Dad wore a tie –
I didn't know he had one –
and even though it wasn't Sunday
mi Mam took off her pinny.
Our lass had bow ribbons tied round her ringlets
and I had to wear mi new school blazer.
We'd shifted tables and chairs
to make room for the photographer.
He brought a three-legged camera
and a cloak.
He hid himself for a minute or two
and then asked
"Ready?"
We said we were and smiled.
He dropped a match onto a little tray
he held by his head
and the room turned so white
you couldn't see a thing,
like waking up in the night
but opposite.
I asked Dad about the light
and he chuckled, saying it was only
a flash in the pan.

The Bearded Lady

Went to Brid Fair at weekend.
What got me was that Bearded Lady.
Dad was chuckling to himself all the time we were in
    there.
Mum dug him in the ribs a few times
but he just kept chuckling.
Outside she asked him what the heck was up with him.
"Nowt," he said.
And laughed out loud.
She asked him again.
"Nowt," he said.

When Mum went off for brandy snap,
Dad whispered that Granny had a better moustache
    than the Bearded Lady.

Appendicitis

I know I aren't well.
Mam thinks I'm skiving but I aren't.
Any road, doctor's come.
He presses mi stomach, feels mi forehead,
listens to mi breathing, takes mi temperature.
I'm in mi pyjamas
and next thing
he's undoing the knot to push down the bottoms.
I've read about funny doctors in the *News of the World*
an' I grab hold of 'is 'and.
"It's all right, old man," he says.
And smiles.
Before I know it his hand's on mi bum,
and there's this sudden pain.
By heck, it does hurt.
Then he tells mi Mam "Acute appendicitis."
Mam starts to cry.

All I can think about is the pain in mi bum.

Gone fishing

I'm out fishing today.
It's boring.
Been sitting on this titchy boat for four hours.
Boring, boring.
I'm sunburnt, been sick.
Embarrassed 'cos I had to pee
over the side of the boat.
The men reckoned they wouldn't look
but they did.
Boring, boring, boring.
Then some excitement!
Thought they'd caught summat,
but their lines were tangled.
Caught nowt.
Bit of fun when Billy chucked up his breakfast.
The blokes laughed.
But it's still boring.
Waved at Wessies in the *Yorkshire Belle*.
Boring, boring.

If they want me to come fishing next Saturday,
I'm off train spotting.

Differences

"I'll show you mine if you show me yours," she says.
I can't believe it.
Alice is the bonniest lass in class
and the smartest.
Why she picked on me I don't know
but I reckon I'll be daft not to go.
The other lads will be narked about it, I know,
so I nod.
"I'll meet you behind playground fence
after school today," she whispers,
and smiles.
I melt.
At dinnertime I tell Mam I'll be late for tea.
She gives me a rocket and tut-tuts about homework.
"It'll soon be July," she says,
"and time for tests."
I don't care about summer exams,
I've got something else to think about.

Alice is there like she said.
I can't believe how different they are,
mine and hers.
Hers is soft and delicate,
mine all hard.
We stay till it gets too dark to see
then we wander home
with even better poems.

A school outing

Old Parky is taking us out today.
We're off to t'Priory.
It's really called St Mary's Church
but all Brid folk call it Priory.
For history we're doing meddy evil stuff
and I thought if there was owt evil it'd be in a church.
I'm right looking forward to it.
I've heard that clock chime ever since I were a nipper
but to hear it at t'church door is great.
It's huge inside with wooden pews
and fancy painted glass as windows.
No-one makes a sound.
Old Parky's already clipped Billy Jones for chattering.
I wonder why God doesn't like noise.
Then Parky chooses six of us to go up the stairs,
past the bells, on to the roof.
It's spooky and cobwebby on the stairs.
All I can see is walls and the boy in front's bum.
After clambering up a ladder
I climb through a trapdoor
and I'm outside.
I can see for miles . . .
all the way to Flamborough Head
probably to Hornsea too.
There's too many trees to see the town though.
I realise where I am and giggle.
Parky's still down below
so I laugh out loud
'cos I know God doesn't mind noisy lads one bit.

A real good day out

Mind you, I was only a lad
and I was mad keen on trains.
I was fed up with Bezzy –
that was where spotters watched the Malton Dodger
    and other local trains.
I'd seen D49s, B1s and K3s there
but I wanted to see a streak.
They were streamliners:
a sloping front and filled in sides over t'wheels
and painted LNER blue,
not like the black hulks at Brid.
Anyway, mi Mam and Dad had to go to York
to meet some of the family.
So we went by train.
By the time we pulled into York
I was nearly wetting myself with excitement.
The station was packed with engines and carriages
setting off for London and Edinburgh.
Then I heard it.
Streaks have a chime whistle all of their own
and one was coming!
Beautiful blue pulled elegant carriages.
The engine was *Mallard* - a record breaker,
and the train was *The Flying Scotsman.*
It was all over in seconds.

I could see that engine
all the way through Granny's funeral.

Neighbours

We've got new neighbours.
Mrs Kirby died and next door was empty for a week.
A family arrived:
Father, mother, and two bonny lasses.
They're from Bradford.
Mother's lip curled.
"Mucky 'ole, Bradford,"
she sneered,
and Dad said summat about "Bloody Wezzies!"
We 'aven't spoken to 'em
and they 'aven't spoken to us.
Mother says:
"If their ball comes into our garden,
don't chuck it back."
But I will.
I mean,
we've to get on wi' neighbours somehow.

Spaced out

Mi Mam and Dad are arguing.
She wants The Archers;
he wants the news.
Something's happened
and he wants to know more.
But Mam says Mrs Dale's worried about Jim.
"Bugger Mrs Dale. And Jim," says Dad.
Mam tells him to stop bloody swearing,
and they both look at me,
but I'm not listening.

Dad has to make do with the radio
'cos we're the only ones in the lane without a telly.
He's fiddling with buttons:
there's nowt but squeaks and beeps.
"That's it!" he shouts
and I'm supposed to believe
the Russians have put something into space.

Eating out

Dad had some overtime pay
so yesterday we had a bus ride,
all the way to Scarborough,
to go on the sands.
Mum said, as a special treat,
we would eat out.
A pal at school
told me he'd eaten out,
at a flash restaurant.
I fancied that.

We had dinner
at the Grand Hotel.
Well, not really.
We huddled under their canopy
and scoffed fish and chips out of the *Evening News*
with salt and vinegar,
raindrops tickling our necks
and a mucky look from the doorman.

Cricket

Mam and Dad have bought me this cricket bat.
It's signed by Denis Compton.
Not a real signature but burned on the wood.
I've to polish the bat with linseed oil every day
to stop it getting too dry.
It's a belter.
I've been practising defending the wash basket.
Daren't take it into the street
where we have a lamppost for a wicket.
Dad'd be mad if the bat was damaged.

To keep my eye in, I've played French cricket
with all my mates on the green,
and with our lass on the sands.
Got quite good at that.
Scored a hundred and thirty last week.
Mind, it was only a tennis ball.

I've to keep my bat for school matches, Dad says.
I'm in the third team at last

and now I'm waiting to bat against
Hymers College.

He's out! I'm in!

I'm back. I got a bloody duck!
Out first ball.

Denis Compton's bats are useless.

Hitler

I don't know about you
but I can't stand kids with ginger hair.
They're always gobby and pushy,
won't listen.
And short-arsed ginger-tops are worst.

Ginger hair and little,
they all want to take over the world.

I'm surprised Hitler has dark hair,
that daft quiff,
and a poxy little black tash.

God knows what he would have been like
if he'd been ginger.

◆

If only Caesar
had been a peaceful Roman.
He would have saved me
from hours of boring homework
and I might have liked Latin.

German lessons

In 'Specky' Watson's form -
never 'class' at grammar school -
I am three of diamonds.
The row in front of the door is hearts,
next one is clubs,
then diamonds,
with the row by the windows as spades.
Front seat is ace,
second is two and so on.
He is flashy with cards:
he shuffles them and cuts them
then shuffles again.
Turns over the top card.
Every boy is quaking.
If it's your card
you recite your homework.
"Three of diamonds!"
"Ich weiss nicht, was soll es bedeuten . . ."
I stumble over the words' foreignness
under his Teutonic glare
but reach the end of the verse.
"Sit, boy," he says and shuffles the cards.
Blackboard erasers fly, detentions are ordered,
extra homework flung at unwilling pupils,
if the recitations fall short of perfection.
But it works.
The first verse of *Die Lorelei*
is imprinted on my brain.

I've no idea what it's about of course.

Errand lad

I hate being errand lad.
There are parcels to deliver
and letters and papers to post.
Wilf Stabler, the foreman, points to a box on a barrow,
and I've to wheel it to the main Post Office.
The barrow looks as though it's been on the railway
but now it looks very sad.
Its iron wheels have lumps missing,
and the box is tied on with Massey Harris string.
The box is an old tea chest
stuffed with papers
rolled up and labelled and stamped.
I wangle it on to the pavement
and start to drag it up the street.
What a row!
The wheels crash down between paving slabs,
thump as they hit the road at junctions.
By the time I reach the Post Office
everyone in town must know about it.
My face shines pink when people look at me.
The post box has just a small slit
and I have to squeeze each paper through.
A bloke in a uniform comes out
and shouts: "What the hell are you doing?"
"Posting the *Chronicle*," I tell him.
He stops me and takes me round the back
to the sorting office where I can leave them in a heap.

Nobody told me about the sorting office.
I might have been to Grammar School
but they grin and tell me I know nowt!

Lossiemouth

Dad was in the RAF at Lossie
and in 1941 Mum took us two kids to live there.
There's a few photos left marked
'Whitsuntide 1941';
that's all I've got,
not even memories.

Just in case

I must be in love
'cos she pushes things out of my mind.
I'm supposed to be taking the dog for a walk
      this morning
but I'm biking past her house.
      Just in case.

Tomorrow I'll volunteer to get mi mum's shopping
'cos she goes to the same corner shop for her mam.
So I'll be there.
      Just in case.

She's called Wendy,
she's nice.
Tomorrow night I'm off to the church social club.
She's a member,
so I thought I'd join.
      Just in case.

But I'm still seeing Nancy at the pictures tonight.
      Just in case.

The first

They say I have to
and I daren't say no,
unless I want a thumping.

So I drag on it.
My head explodes,
I can't see through the tears,
my tongue's stung by a million wasps,
and my throat's like a bonfire . . .
. . . I'm choking.

Billy takes a pull on his,
breathes out like a dragon.
"You'll get used to it," he coughs.

I wish I'd let them thump me!

Read on *Radio Humberside*, Tuesday, 9th January 2007

My father's hands

My father's hands and arms were packed with strength –
he carried printers' formes of steel and lead.
His muscles bulged and strained the whole day's length,
until he stumbled home to welcome bed.

My father's hands caressed my mother's brow
when work was done at end of toiling day.
He stroked her face with loving care; somehow
the love they shared could be expressed this way.

My father's hands rewarded all my good,
chastised sometimes my many errant ways.
My father's hands made all our toys of wood
and cherished us throughout our childhood days.

No longer do my father's hands exist.
I wonder if he knows how much they're missed.

Dad

I've got over not having Dad,
well, nearly.
He was lost, in a plane over Berlin.
Everyone gives me a hug
and says: "Poor little lad."
And my Mum sobs some more.

I don't know what to do when Mum cries.
All I can do is snuggle up close
and put my arms round her,
but that makes me cry as well.

She's brave, though.
She takes washing in so we can keep going.
I wish I could grow stuff in the garden
like Dad did,
just to help.

Sometimes we sit and stare out of the window.
I think she's waiting for him,
even though she knows he won't come.

What will we do when baby's born?

School report

In Form IIa at Oxford Street Junior School -
Term ending 31st July 1945 -
I am nine years, two months,
twenty-seven days old.
Form mistress Mary Marshall
records I am 23rd out of 47,
my punctuality is excellent
and my conduct good.
There are three As,
four Bs and two Cs -
excellent, very good and good.
In the remarks column
my A in English Language
is complemented by
"Very good; steady work.
Tries hard in composition."

It seems a satisfactory report,
although there's a warning
to guard against carelessness.

More than sixty years on,
nowt much has changed.

See me! M. Marshall

First day at the Grammar

My Mum straightens my cap
and gives me just a quick hug.
She's bought me a new satchel though,
and that upsets me.
I know what bigger boys at school
do to "gassy new kids."
With a shiny satchel and a new cap
I'll stick out like a lollipop in a bag of chips.
I meet my friend at the end of the street
and we trudge towards the school gates.
We look at each other but say nowt.
Just past the first few trees on the drive
a sixth former bumps into us.
"Gassy new kids," he laughs.
I'm blushing as I pick my cap out of the puddle.
I keep looking for the fountains like in Trafalgar Square,
the ones I heard they duck you in.
What will Mum say if I go home wet through?
I can't see one, but boys are drinking water
in the corner of the quad.
I bend to have my turn
and another big kid bashes my head down,
smashing my teeth against the spout.

I hate bloody grammar school already.

Shame

I don't know what's happened,
but our lass is having a bairn.

Mam's stopped her going into town
with her friends.

Mam and Dad have been whispering,
but I weren't near enough to catch everything they said.

I think mi Mam worries about what people will think;
Dad said it's nowt to do with anybody else.

Yesterday our lass had to fetch me from school.
Mi Mam was sick
and Dad was at work.

Mam told her to go by the back alleys
and not the main road
because she didn't want anyone from church to see her.

I don't really know why.

Does Mam think our lass should be ashamed
'cos she isn't married?

I was born in May;
Mam and Dad were married at Christmas
the year before.

Shouldn't me Mam understand?

Tandem

Ted Scotter's borrowed a tandem
and asks if I want a ride.
He says: "It's better if you go up front."
He knows about being on the back.

I have to steer and pedal it
just like our normal bikes.

After a few yards,
we've got the hang of it,
and reach the end of the road.
We turn down Fortyfoot
and set off downhill into town.

"Let's get some speed up,"
he shouts,
as he pushes the pedals faster and faster.

We are flying!

When we come to turn the corner
at the bottom of the hill,
we lose control.
I'm steering one way,
Ted the other.

The bushes break our fall,
but the tandem has a buckled front wheel.

Two heads *aren't* better than one.

Mrs Greenham

There's a woman down our street called Mrs Greenham.
And that's all I know, apart from she lives at No.24.
My mother says it's none of our business what she does,
but I'm suspicious.

There's been a lot of comings and goings this week,
a lot of men, all different.
One comes in a car and has a brown briefcase;
he looks out of place round here.
Another comes on a racing bike,
which he leaves leaning on the hedge.
He looks well off, so he won't miss his pump.
But he'll have to push his bike home after I let the tyres
    down.
And then there's that big, fat man with a cigar.
I've seen him twice before.
He's always smiling when he leaves Mrs Greenham's.

The tally man calls on Tuesdays
and there's never a bloke around then, I've noticed.

At weekends there's sometimes a party
and they were playing *Rock Around The Clock*
real loud yesterday.
My Mum was chittering about it
but said nothing could be done.

I thought . . .
If Mrs Greenham had too many men,
perhaps Mum could have one
and then I'd have a Dad.

Frogs

Look, God,
I'm sorry about them frogs last week
We were young and stupid.
It seemed like fun at the time.
All they could do was hop.
What we did was . . .
I'm so ashamed, I'm embarrassed to tell.

We know this unused railway line
in the middle of the wood
just outside town.
The pebbles between the sleepers
are just the right size for catapults.
We whizzed a few stones at the trees and flowers,
then Pete saw something move.
He let fly at it,
and we went to have a look.
It was a frog.
Then another, and more of them.
So we loaded our pockets with pebbles,
and, to make it a bit fairer,
we gave them room to hop.
We aimed to hit them
when they were leaping.
I mean, it would have been too cruel
to do it when they weren't moving.
We hit quite a few;
we were pleased with ourselves.

I don't like frogs particularly,
but I'm sorry we tried to kill them.

Calvary

I didn't want Jesus to die that way.
It wasn't my fault!

All they tell me is that he died for *me;*
that he gave his life to save *me.*
Well, I don't need saving, thank you.
My Dad'll look after me.

How can every little thing I do wrong
put him on the cross?
That was years ago.
How could what I do now
affect what happened then?
It doesn't make sense.

If he *was* the son of God,
why didn't he find another way,
so that he didn't die,
where he'd live to be an old man,
giving us his wisdom so that we'd learn?

I feel guilty.

But then . . . I'm a Catholic.

Sinner

Why should I tell him?
What's the point of repeating them words to a priest?

When Father Brown asks: "Have you anything to
    confess, my child?"
How can I say
I called Ted Walkington "a rotten bugger"
for nicking my marbles?

Have I to tell him I have "impure thoughts"
when I'm watching Miss Marshall's tits bounce in PT?
He's a priest,
doesn't think about them things.
He thinks of Jesus, God and Mary all day long.

I've even overheard him say: "Christ help me,"
when he's practising on the organ,
with that stuck-up choirboy Nigel Smythe.

I bet he doesn't look at Sally Jones
and wonder what she's got in her knickers,
so precious she won't let me have a look.

If I tell him all my sins,
he'll know about them.

And then *he*'ll be a sinner.

Mothers

I can't understand mothers.
You never know how they think.

Mam wouldn't let my sister put lipstick on.
Our Alice was mardy
and sulked all day long,
muttering that she was thirteen.
She's six years older than me,
'cos I was seven last week.

I can't understand Mam.
Especially when she threatened to clip me.

All I said was:
"If our Alice does run away,
can I have her bedroom?"

My Mum

Not one to show affection was my Mum.
For all her life she'd thought the worst of me
but, though we'd fought, it's very plain to see

that on this better day my hour has come
and now I am the man that I would be.
Not one to show affection was my Mum

for in her frosted heart she thought me dumb:
that I could never reach the heights that she
had wished. From manhood back to nursery,
not one to show affection was my Mum.

Railings

Our school had those railings for years.

I remember looking through them
on my first day,
waiting for mi Mam to come for me
at dinner time.
I'd had enough of school by then.

Yesterday men came with roaring blue flames
and cut them down.
When I asked what they were doing
they said: "You're a nosy little beggar."
I think it was 'beggar.'

But I pestered and they said:
"They're for the War Effort."

I thought that was brilliant.
It was worth losing the railings for.

I'm going to be a bomber pilot
so I can get my own back
for them blowing up our Woolies.

I'll dump them railings right on top of Hitler.

Wish list

Today, Miss Marshall asked us what we wished for.
I didn't understand: "How do you mean, miss?"
And she beamed at all us children
saying: "If you could have anything in the world,
what would it be?"
I thought about it,
but I couldn't tell her,
I couldn't even write it down.
I thought about it some more
then Miss Marshall asked:
"Have you finished already, John?"
I'd learned not to lie. I had to say: "No miss."
"Well, write something down, please," she said.
So I did.
I put the words on the paper,
I think they were spelled right.
Teacher asked Pete to read out what he'd written.
He said: "I wish I could be a train driver."
Teacher smiled. "Very nice, Peter."
Sue said: "I wish I had a pony."
Teacher said: "Very nice, Susan."
When she asked me to read,
I wobbled as I stood up
and read out the words on my page.
It went quiet.
Miss Marshall said: "Read it again, Johnny."
So I did:
"I wish my Dad didn't hit me."

Daffies

I picked that little bunch of flowers,
from my very own row,
and was chuffed when I carried them to school.

Dad grew spuds and peas and carrots
to feed a family
but found space for me
to grow daffodils.

Other boys
ripped them from my fingers
and stamped them on the playground.

I don't grow flowers for teacher any more.

Frog spawn

School went on a nature ramble last week.
Teacher showed us things I'd never noticed before:
Different grass, red admirals, dragonflies,
minnows, sticklebacks,
even a heron –
very rare round here, teacher said.
There were flies skating on top of the water,
and bumblebees buzzing.

I liked paddling in Gypsey Race.
My feet were cold in my wellies,
but the breeze off the sea was warm.

Because it was spring
we searched for frog spawn.
We found some in a quiet corner of the stream.
Teacher told us it grew into tadpoles,
then frogs.

I couldn't see that myself
but teacher's supposed to know best.

At home Mum calls it sago pudding.

Firework Night

Me and my brother love Firework Night.
My Dad always buys a few of our own
even though we share next door's.

Catherine wheels are fantastic,
all whizz and buzz.

Roman candles? Wow!
The way they throw that ball of light
into the air.

Rockets are brill.
Light the blue touch paper . . .
and scarper! Quick.
Then whoooooosh! Crackle! Crackle!

Bangers are fun too,
especially that one I let off
just behind our lass.
She wet her knickers with shock.

When we put a big banger
under a tin can,
it nearly goes over the house!

Firework Night.
Jack comes even after the accident last year.
He likes the sounds I think.

Sometimes he gets in the way,
him and his white stick.

Forgiveness

I remember Joe Davis.
"A legend," said my *Wonder Book for Boys*.
I gawped at breasts of African women,
learned Cherrapunji had more rain than anywhere,
was overwhelmed by the splendour of the *Queen Mary*,
envied Denis Compton,
whose Brylcreemed head was everywhere.
I learned about Ayres Rock, Saturn,
and the Humboldt current

I remember that book,
when I hear those names.
Especially the page pierced by a dinner fork thrown
    in my sister's anger.

On that day years ago
she said she hated me.

Every Christmas Day I forgive her,
and wish I could remember what I'd said
so I could say sorry.

Pullovers

Mi Mam's knitting again.
Click, click, click, all the time.
Right through Dick Barton,
and Dan Dare on Luxembourg.
I daren't say owt.
I keep my gob shut
and struggle with the Cantilever Crane
I'm building with my No.6 Meccano set.
Mi Mam's got wool all over the settee
and the table is covered with
brackets, bevel gears, box spanners and bolts with nuts,
pulleys, pinions, plates, perforated strips,
girders - flat and braced -
plus bits and pieces and my screwdriver.
When I've finished,
I'll have a fantastic crane.
When mi Mam's finished,
I'll have another bloody pullover.